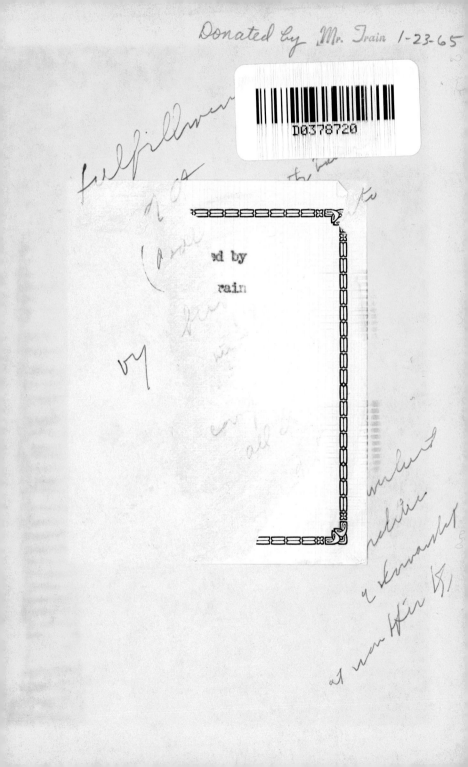

ed by

rain

THE
INWARD
CROSS

THE
INWARD
CROSS

Charles Duell Kean

Philadelphia
THE WESTMINSTER PRESS

Dedicated to
Jane Kromer Kean

CONTENTS

INTRODUCTION

THE CHRISTIAN CHURCH proclaims the cross of Christ as the only hope for our troubled world. If we are to respond to the proclamation, that cross must become an inward cross. It must become the key to our daily experience in every respect. It must not only become our possession; rather, we must be possessed by it to such an extent that we see the whole of life in its light.

People who are struggling with the enormous problems of our day want a sure hope to arm them for the encounter. They want an assurance that behind the difficulties, defeats, and frustrations of the present there is an abiding purpose. The cross speaks specifically to these universally felt human needs, but not in the way men expect. Its good news is the news of death first, and then new life through personal crucifixion.

The cross seems to be a peculiar answer to offer people who are perplexed by the threats of war, who are wondering whether individual personality can have any real value in a technical age, and who are uncertain what role the family has left to play in modern urban society. The cross seems inconsequential, immaterial, and irrelevant. Yet the Christian Church has nothing to say unless the cross is the accepted premise for both speaking and hearing.

The following pages are a meditation based upon the traditional "words from the cross," written in the hope that they may be able to help modern men and women to appreciate a little more deeply the power and wisdom of the cross. The witness of Christian experience is that when the cross becomes an inward event in the hearts of men and women, instead of simply an external happening of long ago, the power and wisdom of God are known at first hand.

The cross has to proclaim its own message. We can talk about it. We can philosophize upon it. We can develop theological systems with reference to it. But the Christian gospel is proclaimed only when men and women are confronted directly with the crucified Saviour of the world, who speaks personally to them — heart to heart. The purpose of this book is to help to set the stage for such a confrontation.

In one sense, this is a Good Friday meditation, because its theme is so completely the event of Calvary. But Good Friday is not just a single day, but the dramatic description of one side of every day. Every decision of both individuals and groups raises the question of the cross.

In another sense, this meditation is appropriate for Lent, because this is the season in which people prepare for Easter. If Good Friday is meant to be one side of the meaning of every day, Easter is meant to be the other side. Participation in Christ's victory requires sharing his Passion. The cross and the resurrection are obverse and reverse of each other, and can no more be separated than can the two sides of a penny.

If these reflections on the cross can help to establish its inwardness, their purpose is being served. They are written in the same spirit in which Fr. George Tyrrell wrote, " Time and again I have been tempted to give up the struggle, but every time the figure of that strange man on the cross sends me back to my work again."

THE TRAGEDY OF HUMAN PRETENSION

"I am crucified with Christ." Gal. 2:20.

THE ROOT PROBLEM of modern times is spiritual. It is not so much that material things loom too large in the thinking of men and nations as that modern man is trying to play God. A titanic spirit of human self-sufficiency competes with the love of God for the loyalty of mankind.

The confusion of the modern world has causes more deeply rooted than are our differences in political and economic thinking. They are deeper than our differences in philosophy and emotional reactions. They are deeper indeed than our fears and anxieties, our suffering and insecurity, our tortured uncertainty.

Here is a spiritual problem with which man does not like to come to terms. Our confused modern world, uncertain as to the prospects of peace and war, the possibilities of domestic prosperity, and indeed perplexed as to the role of the family and the individual in society, would rather evade the underlying issue of man's pretension than face it.

Reinhold Niebuhr once described the root problem in a diagnosis that went behind the tension between the United States and Russia:

" Both obscure the fact that the root of man's lust for power and of his cruel and self-righteous judgments on his fellows is in himself and not in some social or economic institution. If man understands that fact, he can use and refashion political and economic institutions to harness, deflect, or suppress human egotism. If he does not understand it, civil wars arise between those who regard some institution, such as property, as the root of all social virtue and those who regard it as the root of all social injustice " (*The Nation,* March 6, 1948).

When we refuse to face the spiritual problem of our own egotism, we throw up all sorts of smoke screens in theory and activity. We all do. We keep ourselves busy at the things that interest us or appeal to our sense of duty. We defend our prejudices as if we were dealing with simple objective facts. We wax warm in defense or remain coolly indifferent to this or that question, whether it concerns European recovery or how to bring up our own children, and use the occasion as one more opportunity to escape looking into our own hearts.

The tensions that arise in our homes cannot be fully explained in terms of differences of opinion. While practical matters are usually the occasion for conflict, every difficulty has a more serious side. The egotism of the participants is involved, along with practical questions of whether they will spend or save, go here or there, do this or that. Nobody who stops to analyze his own part in an argument can fail to see that the original subject matter is usually left behind at the start, so that the real question becomes one of who is going to win.

Because of the tendency in all human nature to refuse to face adequately the problem of individual and group egotism, it is very hard for us really to be ourselves. Instead, we find it easier, certainly more comfortable, definitely safer, and infinitely preferable, to live in a world of pretensions. We all have moods when we know that even those closest to us — our wives or husbands — do not really know what goes on in our inmost beings, neither the best nor the worst. Most of us would rather not reveal this inmost part of ourselves, or have it revealed in the pure light of day. We would rather live in a world of partial make-believe in which the meaning of our struggles is always distorted. We would rather not face frankly the fact that each one of us by himself is a poor devil who tries to protect himself at the expense of his brother whenever the heat is on.

Behind the insecurity of international relations and the uncertainty of our economic future is the same spiritual problem
of our pretension, falsifying the issues that concern us most
intimately. And unless this problem of pretension is faced,
whatever we attempt is partly corrupted at the source. The
record and results of the San Francisco Conference which
launched the United Nations and the struggle of this organiza-
tion both to survive and to believe in itself are proofs in point.
The story of every family's trials, successes, and failures must
be read in the same light.

The Christian faith proclaims that the cross sheds that kind
of light which penetrates the fog of confused human relations
and reaches the underlying spiritual problems of men and
women. Our perennial human tendency to pretend and evade,
wherever our own egotism is involved, is always present in
every situation, but in the setting of Calvary it stands out
sharply and starkly for what it is.

If Good Friday were but an anniversary of the martyrdom
of a religious leader long ago, it would be a day when we
might well reflect upon the waste caused by human haste, irri-
tation, and fear — but that by itself would accomplish little. If
the cross were but the instrument of execution used by
crueler ages in the past, then it might remind us of the skin-
deep nature of human civilization — revealed more specifically
in our time by the horrors of modern war. But Good Friday
is not simply an anniversary; nor is the cross just a reminder
of an ancient event.

The cross is a tragedy more profound than any written by
the greatest playwrights of the race — Aeschylus, Euripedes,
or Sophocles of old; Shakespeare of Elizabethan England; or
O'Neill, Sherwood, or Anderson today. It is the tragedy written
by the race of man as a whole, with each of us both a writer
and an actor. It is the drama of the terrible contradiction of
our idealism and our actual performance, with our refusal to
face it for what it is, acted out in the presence of God himself.

Every sensitive person is more or less aware of the gulf between his ideal of himself and his actual behavior in particular situations. Parents know the contrast between what they want to do for their children and the way they actually react in times of stress. Husbands and wives, if their marriages have any real stability, have mental pictures of the kind of relationship to each other that they believe they ought to have. If they have any honesty, they know that they betray this in practice, and also each defends himself against the charges of betrayal.

Parents want the best for their children, and yet injure them while sacrificing their own comfort and convenience for them. The nations of the world want peace, and spend both time and wealth in trying to attain it. Yet the peace they seek becomes ambiguous because each nation tries to define it as well as seek it.

The cross is the tragedy that reveals in one particularly luminous event of long ago what is true of all human encounters with reality. The cross is the description of my meeting myself in my own heart and of my relationship with my neighbors. The cross is the tragedy in which the arrogance of human egotism and the futility of human self-sufficiency work themselves out in life.

The cross is the type-demonstration of my own struggle for meaning for my own life, and of our common endeavor to make sense out of our world, because in both attempts we try above all to avoid exposing ourselves for what we really are. But the cross is this utterly frank and realistic depiction of human nature in action only if it is something more.

The cross is a question addressed to me. It asks me, " Do you make your practical decisions of home, and business, and community on the basis of submitting your own egotism to the will of God, as best you can understand it? " From the viewpoint of Christian faith this is the only basis for living meaningfully. The cross asks me, " Are you willing to admit that such a submission can be only by act of faith? " It can never be my personal accomplishment in any fully complete sense.

In this sense the cross is a question addressed personally and immediately to each of us. It is the gateway to salvation only if we accept it freely — knowing that we really die if we accept it. Most of us would rather not die, and we fear more profoundly the death of our own autonomy than we do the death of the body. The way we answer the question decides what kind of relationship we can have to the saving work of God in Christ.

At the first encounter with the cross, men tend to resist it, to reject it. On the one hand, they claim that they see no vital connection between it and their real needs. On the other hand, to the extent to which they appreciate it at all, it seems to make the most unreasonable demands on them.

Nobody has much trouble understanding the ethic of Jesus when his only connection with him is on the moral level. Not everybody agrees with it, although most people admire it as a very noble attitude toward moral problems. Most people who have reflected on it have felt that if the world did live by it people would be a great deal happier than they are now. But when our encounter with Jesus is not simply with a moral teacher but with a cross — a cross addressed to me — then it is a different matter.

Again, while scholars may have their differences of opinion about the historical Jesus, the average man thinks of him as a noble example of kindliness carried out to the fullest extent. We see a warm personality teaching and healing, and living his message in his own life. Most of us wish we could be a little more like him ourselves. Most of us wish more often that those with whom we deal in our homes, businesses, and community affairs would be like him. But when our encounter with Jesus is not simply with the gentle Master of the Galilee road, but primarily with the crucified Son of God — then it is a different question indeed.

There stands the cross: a problem. We have to take it into account when we consider Jesus, and that forces us to face the fact that each of us is continually trying to play God. In one way or another we are continually crucifying others as if they were expendable and we were not — but the cross confronts us with what we are doing in every area of human relationships. It is a problem, because once it is seen for what it is, we are forced to do something about it. If we ignore it, it is because we have chosen to do so. If we evade it, it is because we are deliberately trying to live by short cuts in daily life. If we reject it, it is because we insist on playing God. If we accept it, it is because Christ is our acknowledged Lord. The cross is a problem about which we must do something, and whatever we do will cost us something.

The cross points to the perennial problem that all sensitive, thoughtful people have recognized since the dawn of time. But it points in such a way as to make us look at ourselves and at our various social groups, our own nation, and our human race. And this is a scandal. While we can see legitimate differences between one standard of life and another — between Hitler and Niemoeller, between Tojo and Kagawa, for example, in the light of the cross we can take no comfort in our own accomplishments, even when they are obviously better than are other people's. We have to choose whether or not to trust the love and mercy of God.

The human situation, which the cross so completely describes, has been given a profound modern treatment in Alan Paton's novel, *Cry, the Beloved Country*. Arthur Jarvis, the young Johannesburg lawyer, who worked for justice for the Negro and then was murdered by a Negro burglar, had written in his last manuscript:

" Thus even our God becomes a confused and inconsistent creature, giving gifts and denying them employment. Is it strange then that our civilization is riddled through and through with dilemma? The truth is that our civilization is not Christian; it is a tragic compound of great ideal and fearful practice, of high assurance and desperate anxiety, of loving charity and fearful clutching of possessions." [1]

But when the cross is accepted as a question addressed to me, asking me freely to submit my natural egotism to God's loving will, it becomes a redemptive tragedy in which not only is the problem of human life described in depth but also the direction is pointed out in which the answer may be sought. But that answer cannot be taken for granted. It has to be appropriated by our own personal faith. It has to be the living experience of each of us in his own heart or it will mean nothing.

Whereas Dr. Niebuhr and many other modern thinkers have pointed out the underlying spiritual nature of the problems of our modern world, our agreement with them is only intellectual until we see that this is a way of saying that these problems are rooted in our own hearts. This spiritual problem is not something remote, something general, something abstract, but rather it is my problem. It is I who am the pretender. It is I whose egotism corrupts my own idealism. It is I who poison my relationships with other people by my desire to defend myself and always to appear to the best advantage.

The tragedy of the cross reveals to me, if I am honest enough to admit it, the reality of my own problem in finding life meaningful and glorious. But it also offers me the opportunity to be " buried " with Christ in his death, that I may be reborn with him. No one had more accurate appreciation of the meaning of the cross than did Paul in writing to the Galatians: " I am crucified with Christ: nevertheless I live; yet not I, but Christ liveth in me: and the life which I now live in the flesh I live by the faith of the Son of God, who loved me, and gave himself for me."

The drama of the cross is not simply one of which I am a spectator, even of a depiction of myself and my own motives.

[1] Reprinted from *Cry, the Beloved Country*, by Alan Paton (page 152); copyright, 1948, by Alan Paton; used by permission of the publishers, Charles Scribner's Sons.

We are all actors in it, whether or not we realize it. We may remain in the great mass of the supernumerary chorus, who reveal without knowing what they are doing the agelong problem of the human race defeating its own aspirations by its own pretensions. Or we can be actors who consciously share the cross with our Lord and find it not only the depiction of our own need but also the only way to an answer.

When his cross is not only the symbol of my natural tendencies revealed in their results, but also the agency for reorienting my whole life, then the cross is no longer isolated in history. It is my cross too, upon which my own egotism is finally faced and dealt with, so that I am freed from defensiveness toward life and enabled to live gladly and creatively as a son of God and a brother of the children of God.

If the cross is to redeem my life, it must become the inward cross. It is only as we use the cross to interpret the meaning of our own lives and the problems we face that the Christian gospel really makes a difference in our capacity for living.

Translating the cross from external event to inward experience is the essential task of the Christian faith.

THE GATEWAY OF FORGIVENESS ·

"Father, forgive them; for they know not what they do."
Luke 23:34.

FORGIVENESS is the gateway by which the cross becomes inward. When we accept forgiveness from anybody, we open our hearts to that person's love. The initial contact of the cross of Christ with those whom it reaches is by way of offering the forgiveness of God to those who admit their personal responsibility for the event.

There can be no inwardness of the cross for those who remain spectators. Until we feel some personal association with Calvary, it may be a familiar, moving story, but it has no vital point of contact with us. For the cross to have a redemptive, healing effect upon us, there has to be some kind of real contact between what happened then and ourselves in our world now.

There is such a point of contact in the story of the cross. It is capable of connecting the most casual spectator to the death of Christ — through accepting the word of forgiveness as being spoken from heart to heart. If we hear the word as addressed to ourselves and are willing to accept it that way, the encounter between ourselves and the crucified Lord becomes personal and potentially powerful.

The Christian fellowship throughout the ages has known forgiveness to be the gateway of recognition connecting men and women with the cross, because by forgiveness the meaning of Calvary is seen to have reference to the human heart. We may not plumb all the depths of meaning in the cross, but we can see without too much stretch of the imagination the parallel between our motives and attitudes and the forces that condemned Jesus. Therefore, it does not require too great a moral effort to hear his offer of forgiveness as addressed to us.

Anyone with any basic honesty about himself and his world can recognize that the cross was the result of human nature's acting simply as human nature. The normal actions and re-actions of men and women will continue to do similar things in many ways as long as people remain on the natural level. And high ethical idealism will not change things very much. Only the inwardness of the cross will suffice.

Jesus was not crucified by the bad people of his day, but by the best people — all of whom thought that they were preserv-ing what was good by eliminating what was dangerous. What they did not realize was that their natural tendency to self-defensiveness made it impossible for them to be objective in the matter, and their natural tendency to pretension gave them a distorted view of the problem.

People who crucify others in the everyday affairs of life are rarely sorry, because their act of crucifixion is a defense re-action to eliminate self-questioning. Crucifiers can always ra-tionalize their actions, because their acts are already based upon protecting themselves. The reaction of the victim, how-ever, is usually to return the compliment if possible, with just as much self-righteousness and just as great a feeling of in-jured innocence. But when the response of the victim is one of gentleness and magnanimity, it may lead the sensitive per-son to some re-examination of his own relationship to the problems that concern him, and some awareness of his own lack of self-sufficiency.

Jesus was led out and crucified. As the soldiers completed their cruel task of execution, the condemned man cried out from the cross, "Father, forgive them; for they know not what they do." As you and I hear that cry, we may hear a very magnanimous person, accepting his fate as graciously as possible, yet at the same time showing that he himself was greater than the circumstances that put him there. Any person

whose understanding is able to penetrate the welter of confused motives and defensive reactions in human behavior is
able to rise above the malice and stupidity of others to a cer-
tain extent. All of us may well hope to profit by his example,
as well as by the model of other persons whose magnanimity
of spirit made them master of adverse circumstances — Socrates
drinking the hemlock, Stephen facing the stones at Jerusalem,
or the fictitious Sydney Carton at the guillotine in Dickens'
A Tale of Two Cities.

In other words, our first encounter with the cross of Jesus
Christ may take the form of a very noble example of a very
noble man, whose behavior we might well emulate and whose
attitude under adversity we might well covet for ourselves in
parallel circumstances. Or we may see a deeper meaning to
this encounter. Indeed, unless the deeper side becomes clear,
the cross is but one of the many martyrdoms of the world's
spiritual geniuses that have bloodied the pages of history. It
cannot be our salvation on the level of noble example alone.

Since the cross, for Christian faith, is not simply an event in
history which happened many centuries ago, but more profoundly an event in eternity which repeats itself continually in
my own heart, I should — if I am mature enough to recognize
it — expect to hear these words of forgiveness addressed to me.
Who is being forgiven? Is it just the Pharisees and Sad-
ducees and Roman soldiers and Jerusalem mob of that sad
day so many years ago, or is it every living son of man, whose
natural tendency to defend himself first and think afterward
continually leads him to destroy the best to save himself? Who
is being forgiven? I am. You and I are. We and our whole
sad race are. The power of the cross to change life's meaning
does not become a vital force for us until we see that its lesson
is designed for us, and that the words spoken from it in those
sad three hours are addressed to us.

Life is full of various kinds of lessons about various things.
But there is a difficulty in bringing these lessons home to our
hearts. Otherwise, no matter how true they may be, we never

really understand them and make our own their burden. Each of us can remember occasions in childhood when he let opportunities go by without realizing their meaning for himself, and now from the vantage point of years we see the issue too late and would save our children from the same mistakes. The problem of education is to make the subject matter taught sufficiently vital to be accepted inwardly as well as learned intellectually, otherwise it never really becomes a part of us.

Jesus, on the cross, did not wait for you and me to grasp the inward message for ourselves when and if we discovered it. He began his ordeal of suffering by referring it to us under the heading of inwardness, when he said, "Father, forgive them; for they know not what they do." Forgiveness, to be real, to be meaningful, to be more than sentimentality, requires a meeting of heart with heart. It is not a one-way proposition in which the forgiver alone is moved to action. Forgiveness, to be meaningful, must be accepted by the one forgiven for what it is. And that means inwardness. That means recognition. That means acknowledgment of reality.

When we try to correct our children for some misdeed, more important than any question of punishment or of future behavior is for the parents and children together to share in the same evaluation of human relationships. Otherwise, correction merely becomes a form of keeping order, and future behavior merely becomes a process of staying out of trouble. We don't need parents, only policemen, to put human relationships on that level, and maturity then consists of learning only by the pain-and-pleasure principle, not by spiritual growth through inward appropriation. Parents who are really concerned about their children want them to acquire a set of values of their own by which to measure life. The whole process of correction is the imparting of such values from heart to heart. More important than any questions of punishment or a second chance is the question of interpretation of the meaning of our conduct; unless parent and child share the same evaluation, nothing creative happens. In like manner, unless we share

Jesus' evaluation of the cross, it has nothing very much to do with our lives.

When Jesus asked God to forgive men, he was not only showing that he himself understood the mixture of confused motives — malice, self-righteousness, idealism, and blind loyalty to a great tradition — that led men to condemn him to the cross; he was primarily asking God's help in opening the hearts of all those who participated in that event and in all events of the same spiritual dimension. In praying that God would forgive men, he was by the same token praying that men, that you and I, would be able to accept that forgiveness on the basis of sharing God's interpretation of the meaning of the cross. For us to accept forgiveness means first to accept guilt for what it is, because we are willing to face the facts about ourselves.

We include ourselves among those to whom Jesus spoke because we know we belong to their number. In our own relationships with each other, we react defensively to the pressure of events without thinking the problem through; we hurt each other in our efforts to protect ourselves; we condemn each other rather than admit our own mistakes. And the result is the re-enactment of the cross, through little crosses, where parents crucify their own children, and children crucify their own parents, rather than accept uncomfortable realities. And the world as a whole is torn by men and nations who want the best without an honest acceptance of responsibility for themselves. We need forgiveness.

To understand the meaning of forgiveness means to know that we ourselves can never be spectators in the game of life, but always participants. We never simply hear somebody express generous thoughts toward those who had condemned him, as we look on with objective detachment. Forgiveness depends upon recognition that we too are involved in the problem and need help. We cannot understand what it is to be forgiven unless we know in our hearts the need to be freed from the pressure of our own past mistakes, to be relieved of the burden of our own failures, to be healed of the wounds to our souls that we have helped to inflict upon ourselves.

Forgiveness is the gateway to the inward cross. When we recognize that the words of generous understanding apply not only to those who were present at that particular occasion on the hill outside Jerusalem nearly two thousand years ago, but just as much to you and me who live in another land in another era, then we have taken the first step toward receiving the cross into our own hearts for our own salvation.

Men will never understand their problems if they believe that they are primarily the result of human ignorance. While it is true that if we understood things more fully we could avoid many pitfalls in life, the fact remains that we do not avoid too well the pitfalls about which we already are informed. Man is not so much ignorant or stupid or even willfully malicious, even though he shares in all three traits. Man is blind — self-blinded — because he dares not face himself, lest he pay too high a price for so doing. Man is afraid — afraid of events, afraid of eventualities, afraid of death — but he is never afraid of these things as ends in themselves, even though he often thinks he understands his own fears. Man is really afraid of being exposed to himself for what he is and having to throw himself upon the love of God.

For Christian faith, the cross is the agency by which you and I are able to come to terms with the realities of our own souls and of our world. The first step in the process is that of recognition. To understand that the forgiveness of our Lord applies to us is to make possible a re-examination by us of our own pretensions. Forgiveness involves recognition, and recognition may lead to a new faith.

"Father, forgive them; for they know not what they do." These words from the cross are spoken to everyone who is honest enough to include himself in the number of those who recognize their need of help and know their own share of responsibility for the distress of the world.

CHAPTER

III

THE OUTREACH OF THE KINGDOM

" Verily, I say unto thee, To-day shalt thou be with me in paradise." Luke 23:43.

THREE CROSSES were erected on Calvary, and three men were stretched out to die. We all remember that two of the crosses were for one kind of crime, while the third cross was the punishment for another. We sometimes forget that when the curtain rang down on the drama of Calvary, there were still three crosses, two of one kind and the third of another — but the alignment was different. Through the miracle of divine love, one of the crosses had been shifted from one category to the other. There was no change in the world's eyes, yet the Kingdom of God had included in its outreach a man condemned for robbery and violence.

Two thieves were crucified along with Jesus. The justice of those times used the same occasion to do away with disturbers of two different kinds of peace. Two men were condemned for continuing to threaten the peace of civil society, the safety of property, the maintenance of public order. The third man was condemned for threatening the kind of peace of mind that his neighbors wished to take for granted.

An observer of the event might have said, " Here are three criminals condemned for their misdeeds," as if the situations of the three men were parallel. And that was what an observer was supposed to think, for aside from the details in the written death warrants tacked to the crosses there was no real distinction between them that an outsider would recognize.

The three crosses were alike because the three victims were all condemned for disturbing the peace of society. Mankind always tends to confuse its spiritual peace with problems of material possession, because men always tend to define their security in material terms. Nagging over money matters often symptomizes a more deep-seated instability in a family. The United States has shown a continual tendency to confuse world peace with economic balances.

Society does not know how to distinguish between threats to its normal order — its way of conducting business and handling daily affairs — and the threat to the premises by which it lives. It confuses the two, always regards its prophets as menaces to its social peace rather than realizing that true prophecy destroys an illusory peace of mind.

The early Quakers, with their talk of nonviolence, were regarded as underminers of the peace of England and the North American colonies. The pioneers in medicine and hospital work, and in the care for the insane and those in prisons, were originally resisted not so much for intruding new ideas into the consciousness of a world that really does not like to think as for upsetting the orderly ways of life.

It is a very easy defense to equate questions about our spiritual health with threats to our property. It saves us the trouble of analyzing the situation and facing the facts about ourselves. If we get away with it, our preconceptions remain unchallenged. We are sure that we are right in resisting encroachments on the familiar order of things on the material level, even when we admit academically that some changes ought to be made some day.

Enshrined in the Constitution of the United States and in the Bill of Rights is the " due process " clause which is, among other things, a psychological reflection of the fact that we feel right in defending our property and our systems of administering it from undue interference by a tyrannical state. The " due process " clause has been invoked, however, not only to resist legislative and judicial tyranny over men's families and businesses; it has also been invoked to retard the progress of social improvement by men who did not want to think and who, often for very noble reasons, wanted things left as they were.

The execution of Jesus along with the two thieves was no mere accident. It has come to be, however, much more significant than the fact that the authorities had three condemned people to dispose of and chose one occasion to get the whole business over with. What the kingdom of this world treated as a routine act, however, became an occasion for the demonstration of the outreach of the Kingdom of God. For the principal victim, the wooden gibbet already was a sacrament of the inward cross. The miracle was that one of the thieves came to discover enough of the same reality to die a reborn man.

The execution of Jesus along with the two thieves was an example of the world's two-dimensional thinking, in which everything is considered on the level of time and place, and thus the deeper meanings are ignored. For Jesus the event was rather to be measured by the yardstick of eternity, and one thief was enabled to use the same measuring standard.

The world's judgment as represented in the three theoretically identical crosses is actually a symptom of the fact that men on the defensive against life will choose to confuse threats to their peace of mind with threats to their property, and thus save themselves the trouble of rethinking the direction of their lives. But for sensitive people the question arises whether such an interpretation is altogether accurate. Rather, is there not direct evidence here on Calvary of a basic confusion in human thinking — in the fact that Jesus, the teacher and prophet, was condemned and executed along with two thieves? When we consider the three crosses on the hill, we may well ask whether we do not have the same confusion in our own daily lives.

Is the coincidence of the two crosses merely the result of the way cases happened to come up on the Jerusalem court calendar one day long ago? Here together are the cross inflicted by man's sense of justice against threats to his property and the cross inflicted by man's fear against a threat to self-esteem. Perhaps it is rather a lesson of our own mistaken way of understanding life through our habit of two-dimensional thinking.

Perhaps there is a lesson for us in the way Jesus was disposed of along with the thieves. But there is a miracle for us in the way Jesus, even in the course of dying, was able to associate one of the thieves with himself in a third and more important dimension.

Men tend to judge life solely on the level of history — the succession of events within time and space. Jesus measured life, however, by eternity — the inner meaning of events as seen in the presence of God. The redemption of the penitent thief shows the difference between the two measurements.

By man's usual appreciation of human relationships, physical death is an " iron curtain." To administer physical death as a punishment is called meting out " the supreme penalty," because in a world accustomed to measuring experience solely on the level of history, a quantitative view of life is the only possible view. To write the end of someone's life is to end the significance of his life too.

Whatever theories we may express about life and death, about the love of God and the value of personality, we usually act as if the quantitative measure were the only practical measure of life's meaning. There is no dimension of depth, no element of qualitative judgment, in the way we actually behave, regardless of the way we like to talk. Thus the execution of Jesus and the two thieves was the action of two history-bound men who imagined that by execution they had disposed of the whole business. Instead of seeing death as the symbol of eternity in daily life, they regarded it as the final solution of an immediate problem, and quite missed the point of what was going on.

One of the thieves responded to the situation completely on the surface level. The crowd, in the cruel practice of the times, was adding to the dying misery of the condemned men by taunts and jeers. This first robber responded with curses and then added his taunts to those thrown at Jesus. He was seeking even in his dying moments to keep his connection with the history-bound world which had rejected him for threatening its security. On the level of ordinary existence, he was making the only atonement possible — the way a child who has been picked on at school will naturally try to take the lead in picking on another victim.

The most natural and the easiest way to make one's own life meaningful is to identify it with the prevailing direction of the group. This is what the first thief was trying to do. He accepted the superficial identification of the threat to peace of mind with the threat to peace of property. But since, as a matter of fact, he was not guilty of Jesus' precise offense — whatever it was — he could comfort himself by joining in the general derision of another person whose crime was supposedly parallel. As a result there was no lesson for him in the affair of the three crosses. He had lived quantitatively and he died quantitatively without ever discovering the deeper levels of experience.

But the other thief was different, and as a result he became the occasion of a miracle — the miracle of the transforming power of God's outreaching love. He was probably no more profound intellectually than his companion, yet he sensed the distinction between the spiritual threat and the historical threat. On the cross, he began to think and to live qualitatively, and as a result death for him became the gateway to the Kingdom of God instead of the " iron curtain," since he was willing to accept forgiveness.

The second thief turned to his companion, and rebuked him saying: " Dost not thou fear God, seeing thou art in the same condemnation? And we indeed justly; for we have received the due reward for our deeds: but this man hath done nothing amiss." And turning to Jesus, he added, " Lord, remember me when thou comest into thy kingdom." Jesus replied, " Verily, I say unto thee, To-day shalt thou be with me in paradise."

What had happened was that the cross had become an inward experience for the penitent thief. He was not only crucified physically for his crimes against public order. He accepted freely the crucifixion of his own egotism, by facing reality for what it was instead of trying to defend himself against it. Thus he was able to find the gateway to the Kingdom, as a forgiven sinner.

In his whole life up to date, this robber had been completely at one in the ordinary history-bound, two-dimensional thinking of the world. But he now recognized that the answer was in an entirely different direction from where he had been looking. Instead of life's meaning being found in using today in order to become secure tomorrow, he discovered that it was rather to be found in living today to the full. He became willing to be reborn for tomorrow when it comes, subject to the demands of tomorrow when it announces them. The penitent thief learned that every moment is dying to the past, learning from the present, and trusting God for the future. In such a spirit, every moment is an eternity of God's love — even one's last painful hours on a cross.

The attitude of the penitent thief is needed by every man who would be adequate to meet the real demands of this real world. It is qualitative living that allows one to see the entrance to the Kingdom of God as something worth passing through. Jesus' reply to the man was a recognition of what had happened to him through the miracle of divine love.

Parents, as ordinary human beings, know what it is to measure the meaning of events at home in terms of their own comfort and convenience, or by the attainment of particular objectives by the children if sacrifices have been made for them, or at least by the smooth operation of family details. But only the parent who is willing to die to the independence that was his before his children were born, and who does not try to gloss over the rough spots of today by his expectation of the companionship he will have when his children are grown, can ever live his role completely.

It is human nature to shape our business conduct on the world's ordinary two-dimensional level of satisfaction and rewards — and to feel that some meaningful crown has been won through making a sale, winning a promotion, or receiving a raise. But only the man whose business is marred neither by the survival of adolescent irresponsibility nor by measuring his life by financial rewards — now or in the future — can ever find his job a vocation, and give himself completely to it.

More significant than the death of the penitent thief on the cross was his spiritual death to his own self-centeredness two hours earlier. He discovered then that eternity was within his grasp, and that even he could be included in the outreach of the Kingdom of God. We can discover the same thing to the extent that the cross becomes an inward experience — whether we encounter it in meeting adversity or in the more prosaic setting of the duties of home and business and community.

The man who is humble before the facts of life and accepts reality, trusting God, no longer has to depend on pretension. He may then find each passing moment to be eternity.

IV

THE PATTERN OF THE FAMILY

" Woman, behold thy son! . . . Behold thy mother! "
John 19:26, 27.

FORGIVENESS is the gateway, and when we are willing to accept it without trying to defend ourselves, it is possible to enter the Kingdom of God. We know ourselves within its reach in spite of difficulties, indeed in spite of the prospect of death.

The pattern of the Kingdom is the family. The transforming power of God in Christ is not limited to emergencies. It reaches life's ongoingness as well as life's extremities. And the effect of the inward cross here is to relate people to each other in a new way, the only parallel to which in ordinary affairs is that of family life at its best.

Jesus looked down from the cross and saw two familiar, friendly faces in the largely hostile throng watching the execution. There in the crowd he saw his mother, who had followed him from Nazareth to Jerusalem, and now out to Calvary. And he saw also the disciple whom he " loved." He asked them to take care of each other: " Woman, behold thy son! . . . Behold thy mother! "

To the extent that their relationship to Jesus was more than natural affection, their relationship to each other would reflect it. If their loyalty to him meant sharing his cross, not only in sympathy, but in inward connection with their own hearts, it would provide the basis for that kind of family which is the earnest of the Kingdom of God in daily life.

Surely the bereaved mother would have a new son to take the place of the one she had lost — a son whose whole interest in life was built upon his association with Jesus, so that he could not but represent him to her. And the bereaved disciple would have a new responsibility — since the Master he had served could no longer provide for his own mother, he would do it for him. But this new relationship was not to be simply one of economic necessity, nor even one of transferred affection. It was to be the pattern of all relationships between all people who have shared the cross.

Jesus knew that part of the pain of bereavement is to be no longer needed by some other person for whom one has a unique responsibility, to whom one is tied not only by affection but also by practical duties. Life without functional ties, by which the respect people have for each other is given practical expression in the routine affairs of home and business and community, is life without meaning. But in the deeper sense, while we recognize that there are no real substitutes to take the place fully of those we have lost, the family pattern of the Kingdom of God means the turning of our sense of personal loss outward so as to transform it into brotherly service to others.

Men and women without actual families tend to lose their grip on life unless they acquire somehow a kind of family relationship to others, where they are really needed and know themselves to be needed in practical ways. But here is something more than the filling of that kind of psychological vacuum which occurs when we need to be needed. Here is a new perspective for all relationships to other people, which enables us to find brothers and sisters in a world of strangers, and to find our common faith to be the framework for a family life more real and more enduring than any ties of blood can be.

So Jesus gave to Mary and to John the responsibility of making a home for each other. Since he would no longer need the ministrations of either of them, they would find themselves wanted and useful in serving each other instead. Their relationship would have its real cement in their common love for the man they had served and lost, and it would provide the type-pattern of all human relationships for which the cross is the central factor.

It is necessary for all of us to know that other people need us to make their own lives meaningful. And we need to serve others to find meaning for ourselves. But any old relationship between people won't do. It makes a difference whose dishes we wash. The spirit behind it gives it its quality, and decides what kind of relationship there is. The basis of association transforms duties into creative opportunities enabling those involved to find meaning for their lives.

For Mary and John the spirit behind their association was their shared loyalty to Jesus — a loyalty that enabled them spiritually to walk the road to Calvary and share the cross as an inward experience. Their new association would not be simply one of administering the details of a home — the marketing, the cleaning, and the laundry. Rather, it would be a new kind of family, in which the spirit of Jesus would always be uniquely present and be reflected concretely and specifically in anything either of them did for the other.

As an arrangement made by a dying man for the protection of those he loved and the carrying on of responsibilities to which he could no longer give personal attention, these words from the cross are perhaps good examples for us all, but no more than that. But when they are felt to be spoken not only to Mary, his historical mother, and to John, the companion of the Galilee road, but also to ourselves, then these words take on a more luminous meaning. They are addressed to us as well as to them, and they say something to every person in whose heart is the capacity for concern for others, because through such concern in the spirit of the cross the family pattern of the Kingdom becomes a reality.

These words from the cross ask us about the quality of our relationship to others and the spirit in which we carry it out. Behind what Jesus said to Mary and John is an understanding of the basic pattern of human affairs as God meant them to be. Jesus described that pattern in his statement, " Whosoever shall do the will of God, the same is my brother, and my sister, and mother." He did not begin his ministry with a casual rejection of blood ties and family responsibilities, but rather he extended the same principle to a much wider area of human affairs. This kind of extension is the Kingdom of God in history — this is the pattern as far as it can be applied to human affairs.

The pattern is both the goal at which we are meant to aim and the standard of judgment on our relationships now. Jesus showed completely in his life and in his death what it is to extend the family principle to the whole of mankind. No other pattern will suffice as the framework for human activities of every sort — in politics, in economics, in normal social intercourse. Therefore, the words from the cross that were addressed as counsel to Mary and John, who spiritually shared the ordeal, are questions to us, asking whether we have really accepted the divine pattern of the family for our relationships with other people.

We may admire a mother for risking her life to rescue her children from a burning building, or a father for giving his wife a life-preserver on a sinking liner. But even animals protect their mates and their young. The glory of humanity is in its capacity to extend the family spirit beyond the ties of blood, beyond the claims of personal companionship, even beyond the lines of race and language and nation. Only the inward cross, at least in principle, can make such an extension a reality.

Probably no words from the cross have more direct and distinct application to our troubled world today, where the hysteric fears of men and groups of men are given no lasting relief by any human invention. Systems of international cooperation do not seem to last very long or work very well, in spite of the good intentions of their framers. Systems of industrial relations are always at the mercy of various forces, even though particular managers and union leaders may have the highest respect for each other as individuals.

Behind the uncertainty and anxiety of the world is a question mark raised, not simply by Jesus but, even more directly, by the actual way life works. This question mark asks what pattern prevails for human relationships in the wider circles of group and class and national affairs, and it inquires concerning the kind of spirit by which these relationships are understood. The uncertainty and anxiety of our present world ask you and me whether it is possible to devise any system which, simply as system, will guarantee peace and co-operation between men.

Systems of human relationships do not seem to run themselves very well. Even where self-interest seems clear, the machinery does not work consistently. The generation of the Hague conventions thought that ordinary business common sense would eliminate all wars in the future, and since then we have had the two worst wars in history. Any practical long-range view of our economy shows what happens when any group within it tries to profit at the expense of the whole, because we are all in the same boat — yet the price structure remains a difficulty.

All of us see a need for peace, justice, and co-operation on every level of human affairs. Our all too natural tendency is to attempt to bring in a new age through some ideal blueprint to be superimposed on our homes or our nation. In the political and economic world, this takes the form of an ideal system. Six well-known modern writers have combined their thinking in a symposium, *The God That Failed* (edited by Richard Crossman. Harper & Brothers, 1949), to show why they turned to Communism in the hope that it would answer this need, and how they turned away again when it failed to meet their expectation. And the primary area of failure was in personal relationships.

The lesson of the words from the cross is clear and plain. We are told that only where the divine pattern, the family, is the basis for human relationships can there be any lasting peace and co-operation. Even enlightened self-interest will not avail. Systems of administration, no matter how sound on the basis of social engineering principles, are not enough. We all know that, even in spite of our experience of tension in our homes, the family pattern is on a higher plane than any other human association we may have.

Even with its shortcomings in practice — since every husband and wife is an individual human being with egotistical reactions — the family still stands as a living contradiction to the prevailing temper of this or any other age. In spite of the conflicts that arise between parents and children in the best of homes, every family that has any reality to its existence demonstrates that mutual love is the real framework for its actions. This is because a family involves not only obligations but also forgiveness, not only privilege but also creative relationships.

The problem of the modern world is to take the spirit of family loyalty, which all of us know to some extent, and make it the pattern for our industrial, national, and international life. The alternative is chaos and destruction — not only of the fabric of civilization but also of the souls of men. Only when the words addressed to Mary and John are applied to all human relationships can they be placed in the kind of perspective that offers realistic hope to the world.

Yet we may know very well what we ought to do, and not always do it. We may know that the future, not only of Western civilization but of the destiny of man, depends upon a new spirit's being infused into the structure of human relationships at every level, but we don't see it infused, and we do not ourselves help its coming. When our functional relationships to each other are not clear, it is hard to give them a noble expression except in words, even though we know we should be better off if we did.

When Jesus spoke to Mary and John from the cross, he would have wasted his breath if all he had done was to appeal to them to co-operate with each other in the future. The family spirit depends first of all upon a shared loyalty, which makes it possible for the members to respect each other and to forgive each other. One of the reasons why family life itself seems so insecure in our modern society is that so very often there has never been any spiritual cement to hold together the young man and the young woman who were once infatuated with each other. But Jesus offered Mary and John a sense of family based upon loyalty to him — not simply to himself as an individual, but rather as a person who lived a point of view. The spiritual cement for that new family was to be the cross itself.

For our modern world, Jesus' offer still holds. In the setting of the cross, he says to every family, " Husband, behold your wife; wife, behold your husband; parents, behold your children; children, behold your parents." In the setting of the cross, he offers this kind of spiritual cement, the bond of union for effective family life, to all other human relationships — in business, in community life, in race relations and international affairs. It is not a new law that he offers. It is not a simple solution of technical problems. Rather, it is that kind of point of view of man toward his fellow man which enables each person who holds it to forgive as he himself is forgiven, and to forgive because he is not concerned about defending himself against the invasion of his own ego.

In ordinary human relationships between husbands and wives, this spiritual cement of the inward cross is available. And the same spirit of common loyalty can be extended to other problem areas of human relationship in this troubled world. Where we are on the defensive against each other, the appeal of higher unities is not very powerful. When we have to pretend to self-sufficiency, it is hard to let ourselves be ourselves with others, yet without such honesty there is no unity. But the cross transforms our understanding of ourselves, freeing us from the need for defensiveness, releasing us from pretensions about ourselves, so that we, like Mary and John, may accept the divine pattern for human relationships and make the spirit of the family the basis for our approach to problems of world order.

CHAPTER V

THE ANCHOR IN REALITY

" My God, my God, why hast thou forsaken me? "
Mark 15:34.

THE INWARD CROSS makes it possible for us to plumb the depths of life because when our lives are understood in terms of it they are anchored in reality. Therefore, neither the long, dull, dry periods of humdrum experience nor the bitter shocks of desperate, hopeless situations can cut us loose from our foundations. We may be helpless as the world measures things, but where the inward cross is the central factor in our lives, we are never completely at the mercy of circumstance.

Through facing our need for forgiveness, we come in contact with the outreach of the Kingdom of God. At least we can discover, if we will, that the long, strong arm of his love takes the initiative, no matter who we are or what we have done. To encounter the Kingdom of God with reality is to know also that the pattern of the family is the norm for all human relationships regardless of their size and function.

The acid test of the soundness of our lives, however, is what happens when we face despair, when nothing immediate seems able to make the slightest difference, when frustration and defeat are inevitable, when there is no objective justification for keeping up the struggle of life. And it is precisely here that by finding the cross in our own inward experience, we discover our anchor in God's eternal reality. The anchor chain is our continuing identification with the family of his children in spite of every possible influence to the contrary.

The purpose of crucifixion was to allow men to die in double misery, because to the anguish of the tortured body was added a deliberate psychological isolation from other people. Along with physical pain, the condemned man had to face social rejection in a form he could not evade, as he slipped toward physical death. As the hours dragged by on Calvary, the three victims could not help realizing that they were losing spiritual contact with their fellow men in an experience that had no meaning. Here in dramatic form was the acid test which determined whether a man had a faith to hold on to, because here is the deepest loneliness with a cutting edge.

Pain always isolates, because the sufferer feels it as a unique pressure on his soul as well as a racking strain to his body. It always tends to be a pressure that others cannot share and cannot understand, so as to isolate the sufferer in bitterness from man and the universe. Social rejection always isolates too, because the victim feels himself regarded as an outcast whether he knows himself to be guilty or innocent. Being an outcast is spiritual loneliness as well as social discomfort. Death always isolates, because we are born alone and die alone, and while death is the eventual common experience of mankind, the individual encounter is always solitary, with no other person able to ease it by sharing it.

Then one of the sufferers cuts through the wall of spiritual isolation by crying out in the ancient faith of Israel those words from the Twenty-second Psalm: " My God, my God, why hast thou forsaken me? " Here is a cry of healing, which penetrates the very depths of despair and digs yet deeper to the bedrock of reality. Here is an affirmation, arising out of the penitence of Israel, to enable a man to place his hope in God's eternal righteousness.

To hear this cry from the cross simply as a set of words is to miss their depth. Without appreciating their association in Jewish faith, they sound simply like unrelieved anguish of soul and body. But this phrase is taken from the General Confession, so to speak, of the Jewish Church. It is indeed a genuine admission of the deepest spiritual misery, but even more it is an affirmation of an even deeper faith transcending misery.

Jesus used the faith of Israel to bridge the gulf of isolation between himself and God, and himself and his fellow man. Psalm 22 is a Day of Atonement psalm, when the solidarity of Israel is dramatized by the penitence of every Israelite. On the Day of Atonement, every loyal and pious Jew beats his breast and takes upon himself moral responsibility for the suffering of his people. His own personal experience is made to be the bearer of the destiny of Israel, and his own personal hope to focus the general expectation of his nation. The liturgical expression of the mood is in these words: " My God, my God, look upon me; why hast thou forsaken me? why hast thou put me from thee, and art so far from me and the voice of my complaint? "

This cry from the cross was both the deepest and most poignant expression of Jesus' own personal need and at the same time a description of faith's answer. By the use of these words, Jesus identified himself with Israel, the chosen people of God in a spiritual sense, and by the same token identified himself with the crowd at the foot of the cross, with the people of his day, and with all men everywhere who acknowledge themselves subject to the law of God.

These words from the cross are an identification through faith with God's purposes for man. They are not a grim defiance of rejection and isolation. They are not a capitulation of the human soul that has taken all that it can stand. Rather, here is Jesus of his own free action identifying himself through humble penitence with the very men who had condemned him and by that act finding an anchor to reality to enable him to endure his own suffering, and at the same time by the same means using his cross to provide meaning for the lives of others.

Therefore, this cry has become the great classic acceptance of life, the great affirmation of that kind of human solidarity which is utterly realistic and therefore truly creative. Certainly it grew out of the experience of rejection and isolation, and certainly it recognized the forces of pain, social rejection, and death for what they were. Here is no ignoring of suffering, but here is a definite statement that pain, social rejection, and death cannot say the last word about life. They can be bridged honestly through penitence. They can be made opportunities for the discovery of a new meaning for all experience.

The English author D. R. Davies has pointed out that the one way in which all men are alike is in the fact of sinfulness, and that this very fact of being united in this way makes all other forms of unity impossible. Our pretensions to self-sufficiency, to being the ultimate authority for our own lives, to being the final arbiter of significance for ourselves, are shared by every other living person. Yet this common fact raises barriers between us and any person who, rightly or wrongly, appears to threaten the estimate we prefer to hold of ourselves.

The need to defend ourselves in those practical areas where we demonstrate what we regard to be life's meaning — in our homes, in our businesses, in our community relationships, and in national and world affairs, both as individuals and as groups, continually makes all co-operation tentative. We will work with others so long as we do not feel ourselves threatened, and when we are endangered, then no matters of practical efficiency or logical process mean very much to us. We defend ourselves first of all, regardless of whom we hurt by word or deed, and the old problem of humanity — the problem of Cain and Abel, the problem of the Tower of Babel, the problem of civilization in every age — is given one more demonstration.

While we may blame the policies of other nations for the international uncertainty that prevails today, any honest appraisal of the facts shows that our own national hands are not clean either. This does not mean that there are no significant distinctions between our tradition and that of Russia, for instance. What it does mean is that our national self-righteousness adds to the very problems we would solve, and prevents us from facing them adequately. In the same way, many a husband or wife has found that the necessity to defend his or her own rightness, as well as to persuade the other to do something, has made a domestic difference of opinion a tremendous difficulty to overcome. Many parents are both torn and confused by the behavior of their adolescent children because differences in point of view about specific problems, such as the time to come in or when to use the car, carry overtones of criticism which they refuse to face. And the shoe can be put on the other foot in these parent-child problems. In other words, wherever men's interests and desires conflict, we find not only divergent policies but also individual and group selves on the defensive, and consequently there are barriers raised that reason cannot break down.

Most arguments are fruitless because the subject-matter under discussion is not really so important to the arguers as is the estimate of himself which each one feels he must protect. And the longer the debate goes on, the more definitely this aspect increases in significance. We are alike in our egotism. We are alike in our tendency to pretension. We are alike in our assertions of autonomy. Consequently we tend to be on the defensive against each other in practical matters, with the result that misfortune and frustration isolate us in loneliness. The easiest defense is to isolate our critics, where that is possible. The easiest assertion of our own virtue is by trampling on the pretensions of other people.

Under such conditions life can never be truly accepted for what it is, and all human relationships must be carried on in a partial atmosphere of make-believe. The truth is, however, that in this world of defensiveness and pretension there is no real peace — neither peace of circumstance nor peace of mind. Life is not accepted for what it is, nor can it be on these terms.

Jesus broke down the wall of isolation, as far as his own heart was concerned, by refusing to assert his virtue over against the power of the crowd which had rejected him. Instead of a defiance which would have carried the barriers between men on to the end of life, he broke them down by asserting the only basis of identification which is universally true, and which every honest person must admit when confronted with the facts. Jesus cried out from the cross, " My God, my God, why hast thou forsaken me? " using Israel's expression of humble penitence to make him at one with all men as all men really are.

The plain facts of life reveal that, while we may never achieve a perfect world, we do not even halfway try to build as good a world as we can, because we will not give ourselves to each other without reservation. But Jesus refused to remain in isolation. Unlike the way most of us might act, he refused to try and soothe injured feelings by wrapping himself in a cloak of self-righteousness. Therefore, where our misfortunes and frustrations — of illness, of criticism, of the death of someone we love — tend to embitter us and leave us that much more cut off from the fellowship of God's children, he made the cross itself an occasion for uniting men.

Jesus accepted life for what it was, and acknowledged the realities about himself as a man, and therefore the sting of bitterness was drawn. And, to the extent that the cross becomes an experience of our hearts too, we find that our relationships to life are likewise transformed, and we too can accept reality and live creatively. We cannot live in this real world, and be adequate to the challenges laid upon us, if we must remain guiltless in our own eyes regardless of the facts, if we have to protect our own estimates of our own importance.

Again Arthur Jarvis' essay, in Paton's novel, is an excellent illustration of the way a sensitive soul wrestles with this problem in the setting of the concrete issue of race relations:

" I am lost when I balance this against that, I am lost when I ask if this is safe, I am lost when I ask if men, white men or black men, Englishmen or Afrikaners, Gentiles or Jews, will approve. Therefore I shall try to do what is right, and to speak what is true. I do this, not because I am courageous or honest, but because it is the only way to end the conflict of my deepest soul. I do it because I am no longer able to aspire to the highest with one part of myself, and to deny it with another." [2]

When the cross becomes the basis by which we can honestly identify ourselves in humble penitence with mankind, admitting our share in responsibility for our sufferings and the sufferings of the world, then we can meet men on a level that undercuts pretension, and where we all may be one. The inward cross alone gives us that orientation of life which makes possible a creative approach to the problems of our own hearts and of our world.

[2] *Op. cit.* (page 171).

VI

LIFE'S CONTINUING STRUGGLE

" I thirst." John 19:28.

L IFE involves struggle. That in a real sense is what makes it alive. It cannot be reduced to an automatically operating formula, no matter how accurate our understanding of ourselves and the world may be. Life involves struggle in the sense that the concrete demands of our homes, communities, businesses, and world are what test our faith. The physical and material side of life provides the context for making the cross our own inward experience. This side of affairs is real — it is not meant to be ignored or evaded or simply risen above. In a more profound way than he knew, Karl Marx was right in talking about " dialectical materialism," because life consists of the interaction of spirit and matter in the course of real events involving real people.

The cross points up the reality of struggle as sharply and obviously as it can be done. It provides us with an interpretation of the struggle of life in which faith is tested by concrete, physical circumstance. The cross was a physical ordeal. It was meant to be one. It was a concrete demonstration of man's fiendish ingenuity in devising horrors for his own kind. While humanitarian movements have, by and large, made the treatment of condemned criminals more kindly, men still inflict crosses in subtler and more socially acceptable ways upon each other in the course of life's ordinary affairs; and when a man has been broken on the wheel of life, he is left, as often as not, to spend his remaining days in bitter uselessness.

The cross was a physical ordeal for Jesus. It was designed to make a condemned criminal look forward to his own death as a release from prolonged agony. Bone and muscle and nerve can stand just so much, because that is the way man is made physically. And the strain told upon Jesus just as it would tell upon anyone else in his predicament. One cannot struggle long without showing it, and even a one-sided struggle like the physical ordeal of the cross could not but provoke ordinary human reactions. So Jesus cried out from the cross, "I thirst," because that was the natural physical expression of one who had been under a prolonged physical strain.

Yet there was more to that cry than the simple and factual statement of thirst, true as it was. The ordeal of the cross was not simply the subjection of a man's body to see how much pain it could stand. In the case of the two thieves that was about all there was to it, because the pattern of cause and effect had worked out in their cases according to the theory of justice then prevailing. But Jesus had gone to the cross as an act of faith, and just as his body was subjected to the agony of physical torture, so the whole prolonged process was one of testing for his spirit. It was not that a change of mind on his part would have done any good that late in the day, but rather that under such circumstances one could not help asking and asking again whether the price was worth it.

It is one thing to face an ordeal in intellectual contemplation, counting the odds and then going ahead with resolution. It is another thing to face a test once the heat is actually turned on. The spiritual problem of the Garden of Gethsemane, where Jesus had prayed, "If thou be willing, remove this cup from me: nevertheless, not my will, but thine, be done," could not be disposed of once and for all. It had to be worked out over again in the context of hard reality.

When you and I contemplate the cross, and hear Jesus speak, we may recognize easily enough that his expression of thirst shows his spiritual as well as physical ordeal, and the matter may end there, as far as we are concerned. After all, it is true that every physical problem we encounter tests the faith by which we live, but for people who are not very clear about their faith it is hard to see any vital connection between their experience and their philosophies, such as they are. But we may stop and listen a little more profoundly, and notice that the Christ on the cross is not only demonstrating a human reaction to prolonged strain. He is also speaking to us in such a way that where our ears are not deafened by our own pretension to importance, to virtue, and to knowledge, what he has to say has significant bearing on our lives.

One of the most natural ways by which men try to make life easier for themselves is by living in two worlds at once — the one the world of ideas, and the other the world of practical affairs. As long as the two are kept separate, one's own virtue is not in danger, one's own understanding of his own wisdom is not exposed to ridicule, one's own assertion of importance is unchallenged. For many people religion is thought of as a kind of escape from life's pressure. For other people, what happens in the world of affairs is supposed to be unimportant as long as one's heart is in the right place. For still others, this world of business and politics and activity of all kinds is the only reality there is, and what a man thinks doesn't matter. In any event, here are two worlds — because each of us is, at one and the same time, both a thinker and a doer. As long as we do not have to relate the two sides of our natures too precisely, life seems to work along all right.

But once we are under pressure, our faith and our activity refuse to stay separate. When we have to wrestle with a decision upon which the whole future of our lives depends, it is not a matter simply of choosing between alternatives. We also have to answer for ourselves questions about what is worthwhile and why. If a price is involved, its significance has to be measured against something to determine whether it should be paid or not. If in choosing one direction, we must turn our backs upon other possibilities — as when a man chooses to change his job — we want to feel sure we have not made a mistake.

The fact of the matter is that man's physical needs and

spiritual problems are bound up in each other all the time. If we discover this only under pressure, there is little we can do about it, because the fact of pressure itself limits the possibilities — the decision must be made by tomorrow morning, for instance, and there is no more time available. The time for a family to get a working philosophy on the subject of death is not while making arrangements for a funeral, but beforehand. The reality tests our faith, but very seldom offers us much opportunity to discover an adequate faith right on the spur of the moment. If Jesus had not worked his own faith out — in the temptations in the wilderness, with his neighbors in the Nazareth synagogue, on the highroads of Galilee, and finally in the Garden — he could not have met the ordeal of the cross creatively. The cross tested his faith. It was not the occasion for inventing it. And no one can have an adequate faith for living as long as he tries to live in two worlds at once.

The great Swiss theologian, Karl Barth, tried to make a virtue out of living in two worlds at once — being concerned with man's loyalty to God at the expense of paying sufficient attention to the problems of the world around him. The result was that Barth, who was teaching in Germany, was quite unprepared for the advent of Hitler, and eventually lost his job and was expelled from the country. It was only when World War II was actually under way, after Dunkirk, that this great modern thinker, who had done so much to clarify our understanding of the Bible, realized that what he had to say would mean very little in a Nazi world. In an essay entitled " The Letter to the English " he came to the practical recognition that faith and life are related, and that a Christian understanding of the dignity of man was fundamentally incompatible with Nazi success. The outcome of the war, he decided, did make a real difference. Faith and life could not be separated.

The reality of struggle is that it tests our faith. Without convictions by which to stand, our ordeals are meaningless and life is merely a succession of confusing and often painful episodes. But with faith, worked out with honesty, rooted in humility, grounded in penitence, every problem we encounter is one more opportunity for victory.

In T. S. Eliot's play *The Cocktail Party,* there is an illustration of this understanding. Sir Henry Harcourt-Reilly, the psychiatrist, is talking to Edward and Lavinia about the death of a mutual friend, who had been martyred by savage South Sea islanders when she stayed behind at her post at a mission hospital, taking care of the patients. She was crucified over an anthill.

" REILLY: That way, which she accepted, led to this death. And if that is not a happy death, what death is happy?

" EDWARD: Do you mean that having chosen this form of death, she did not suffer as ordinary people suffer?

" REILLY: Not at all what I mean. Rather the contrary. I'd say she suffered all that we should suffer in fear and pain and loathing — all these together — and reluctance of the body to become a *thing*. I'd say she suffered more, because more conscious than the rest of us. She paid the highest price in suffering. That is part of the design.

" LAVINIA: Perhaps she had been through greater agony beforehand. . . .

" REILLY: That shows some insight on your part, Mrs. Chamberlayne." [3]

Every man, as a matter of fact, lives by some kind of faith, whether it is clear or not, whether he uses any particular form of words or not. The appeal from the cross is not for one to live by faith, but to live by that kind of faith which alone will enable us to make sense out of the problems of our hearts and of our worlds. The faith of Jesus Christ is not presented because it is theoretically a concise and logical description of how life ought to be. It is presented only because it is that relationship by conviction to men and nature and above all to God which enables you and me to meet whatever comes with confident purpose.

[3] From *The Cocktail Party,* copyright, 1950, by T. S. Eliot (page 184). Reprinted by permission of Harcourt, Brace and Company, Inc.

There is no religious solution to life's problems which is unrelated to the historical situations in which we find ourselves. The Early Church rejected mind-over-matter interpretations of life as heresy. On the other hand, men do not find their answers to life's problems simply in the satisfaction of their material needs. In the Christian understanding, the issue is one of the spirit in which and by which we address ourselves to the problems of a real world — poverty, war, injustice, fear — not as ends in themselves, but as means by which we bear witness to our conviction that the love of God is the strongest power there is.

The inward cross, whereby our pretensions are eliminated, and through which we frankly relate faith and history, transforms our relationship to this world of necessity. As Jesus cried out, "I thirst," in that supreme test of his own living conviction about life's purpose, so also we are prepared to demonstrate our faith through struggle against those influences which contradict our understanding of life's essential meaning.

CHAPTER

VII

OUR PART IN VICTORY

" It is finished." John 19:30.

THE CROSS reverses the world's normal system of values. If we share it, so that it becomes an inward cross, it must reverse our understanding of the relative importance of things too. But only when the cross is inward does this contradiction occur.

Death becomes the basis of new life — in the light of the cross. But that is not so surprising when we see that, in the same light, our relationship to God and man is really founded on our admission of a need for forgiveness rather than upon our achievements. Neither is it strange when we remember that the family is the pattern for ongoing living rather than some more mechanical and more efficient method of organizing human action.

In the light of the cross, we discover our anchor to reality by plumbing the very depths of despair and finding an even deeper strength to which we are tied through identification with the children of God. In the light of the cross, we find our joy in the continuing struggle with the intractable yet concrete factors of the physical world, rather than in the elimination of tension.

The cross is a contradiction of the way the world looks at life. But that is its power. The cross in this sense is rooted in God's scheme of things, not in man's. For men, crucifying others is a way of externalizing problems so they can be disposed of and forgotten. In God's purpose, the free crucifixion of our own egotism through faith in Jesus as the Christ is what gives us a share in his victory.

The cross turns sadness into joy. The cross turns suffering into peace. The cross turns despair into confidence. The cross turns defeat into victory. The world cannot understand this. Nobody can until the cross becomes inward.

As the end of the three-hour ordeal on Calvary drew to a close, Jesus stated calmly and quietly, " It is finished." By the world's standards these words might well appear to be a surrender. As we usually size things up, these words seem to indicate that Jesus knew that he had done all he could but that it still was not enough. The battle was about over, and now there was no chance at all of winning.

But the world, which always makes that kind of estimate of success and failure, based on tangible, objective results, has always misunderstood the cross. The influence of organized Christianity has raised the symbol to a high place, where it is venerated without being accepted and honored without being appreciated. Its standard is just not used to measure the ordinary affairs of life.

The world only heard Jesus' words. Since it does not, as a rule, look at life through his eyes, it cannot appreciate very well his meaning. But from Jesus' point of view, the cross was the beginning of God's victory, right here in human affairs, wherever men of faith are able to understand the meaning of their lives without pretension and without defensiveness toward each other.

From Jesus' point of view, the words, " It is finished," are the announcement of the victory which God can always win through lives that are really given to him. But they can be understood and accepted as such only by those who in their own hearts share his faith. We cannot hear him speak these words if we have the world's ears. Christian conviction denies the validity of the world's measure of defeat and victory.

As the end of the three-hour agony drew to a close, Jesus could feel himself growing weaker. He was already partly numb to the pain as nature's anaesthesia began to take over. By every ordinary human standard he had been defeated. The authorities had condemned him and executed him and now they could start forgetting him. The crowd had misunderstood and rejected him, then had made his execution the occasion for a spectacle, and now were drifting away bored.

Jesus' own disciples had been badly confused. Only one was present on Calvary, and it is hard to tell how deeply even he had appreciated the meaning of events. The others had scattered no one knew where, while Peter, their most voluble spokesman, had the previous midnight denied even knowing his master.

We also are spectators who miss the point of what we see unless we hear Jesus' words addressed personally to us. When we hear him say, " It is finished," the question must arise as to what is finished. If it is merely his own ordeal as a sufferer on a cross, of which we are spectators for the moment, then we show that the cross is not in our hearts. It is no measurement for us, only for Jesus. On the other hand, if we hear these words as a description of victory, then our eyes are open to a whole new view of life's meaning, in which we may share, and in which the world's standards of success and failure are shown to be false and misleading.

We always have to contend with frustration and always will, because the struggle for meaning can never be disposed of once for all. It is our natural lot as human beings to strive for what we believe to be worth the effort and then to have our strivings subjected to the test of frustration — either the frustration of victory, where we win and find that what we have won has lost its glitter, or where we lose and find our own estimates of our own importance called in question.

We are always wrestling with the problem of frustration in a world that remains obdurate no matter how many secrets we may bring to light, no matter how many people may admire us, no matter how confident we may be about the value of what we are doing. The man who is a stranger to frustration, to questionings in his own heart as to the value of his own life, is the man who has not lived as a man.

We all desire a perfect world, although we may differ about its details. We all desire to have the circumstances of our lives reduced to order. We all desire to have the tensions of our hearts relaxed. The natural measurement of victory is therefore by results in these areas. Economic prosperity means security, or does it? Personal popularity means happiness, or does it? Recognition by the world for what we have done means success, or does it? Is there any measurement of life's meaning that is safe from questioning? As soon as we have found one, it begins to wobble if we look at it closely.

As a matter of fact, success as a measurement of a complete life is awfully hard to define. We can tell who wins a game by the score, but sometimes the defeated team has actually gotten more out of a football game than the eleven who won it. We can set some goal to attain in business and attain it, but there is no guarantee that it will mean as much in possession as it did in prospect. In other words, the meaning of success — or the meaning of failure — is never objectively clear and obvious.

You and I live and struggle in a world where life goes on. We are never in a position simply to cash in while we have winnings and retire from the game of life, and the next hand may reverse our patterns. Is the United States today a successful nation? Yes, in the sense that we have emerged on the power-controlling side from two world wars, but has success any meaning, has victory any enchantment, when the unsolved problems mounting up today deprive our past accomplishments of practical glamour? As a matter of fact, victory on the level of history is a relative thing and varies in meaning according to the point of view from which it is looked at. Which would we say was the victor in ancient Greece — the Athenians, who lost their empire but bequeathed to us a heritage of art and philosophy which we still use, or the Spartans, who defeated them in war and themselves disappeared a generation or so later with no legacy to speak of? Which would we say was the victor on Hampstead Heath in England — the re-

actionary powers of the Medieval Church, which burned
Cranmer and Latimer and Ridley at the stake, or the Anglican
Church, which still uses the stones of liturgy these martyrs
built into its foundations? To whom would we give the palm
of victory in India — to Gandhi or to the man who shot him?

The meaning of success, in the last analysis, depends upon
the perspective in which we place human affairs. The meaning
of victory depends upon our understanding of life's purpose.
There is no such thing as a self-explanatory, objective success.
There is no such thing as a victory without a frame of reference of some kind. The rewards of life are actually measured
by the faith by which we live. The world that crucified Jesus
showed that its faith had to do with matters of immediate
prestige and honor and popularity, and that defeat meant rejection then and there. But the world was badly confused, because the historic event represented that kind of mixed-up
thought and action by which men who have to pretend and
who have to defend themselves from threats eliminate dangers
to their imaginary success.

The lesson of the cross is that the measure of success and
failure is ultimately beyond history. In our daily lives we
struggle for what we believe to be important, but the struggle
never ends, and even when we as individuals leave the scene,
the last word has yet to be said on any important subject.
History is the area of cause and effect, of trial and error, of
challenge and response, in which we demonstrate the faith by
which we live without any opportunity of adding up a final
score to show where we stand for all eternity.

If our happiness is to depend upon the attainment of un-
qualified success, we shall never be happy, because there is no
such success available. If our lives depend for meaning upon
the winning of victories that are complete in themselves and
leave no doubt as to the value and importance of our contribu-
tion to life, then we shall always have to wrestle with the problem of meaninglessness without any assurance of the outcome.

Where the cross becomes the experience of our hearts, however, we have an entirely different relationship to life, and consequently an entirely different basis for measurement. Our salvation is in our effort to live God's will, as best we understand it, not in success by any external standard whatsoever. " It is finished." Life's completeness is reserved to God. It is never ours. We can do only the best we can with what we have where we are trusting him. But from the viewpoint of the inward cross that is enough. Frustration and defeat no longer threaten those whose pretensions have been crucified.

VIII

TRIUMPHANT FAITH

" Father, into thy hands I commend my spirit." Luke 23:46.

THE EFFECT of the inward cross is triumphant faith. If Jesus is our Christ in the sense that we share his cross through our own personal commitment, we have a relationship to life's underlying reality which is what all men are seeking, whether or not they know it. Here is confidence. Here is strength. Here is power. Here is the peace of God.

But what we seek can be found only on God's terms, and that means the crucifixion of our own egotism in the practical areas of life where we make decisions and are associated with other people. The inward cross is the secret of triumphant faith when Calvary is found in our own offices and homes. It is in these situations that God's will is to be done as far as we are concerned. Therefore, it is here that we find our lives in losing them.

There has been a lot written in recent years about the number of people who say they believe in God. In one college, a survey reported that nearly the entire student body claimed to have such a belief. Christianity, however, is concerned with something more specific, more dynamic, more concrete. The only kind of God worth believing in is the Creator of heaven and earth who is revealed in the life and death and resurrection of Jesus Christ, which we dare to believe we share.

Triumphant faith is not a list of opinions that we hold resolutely despite opposition and disagreement. Triumphant faith, in the Christian sense, is identification. We know God the Father at first hand, because we see life, as it were, through the lens of the cross. We see ourselves in this setting as " I's " which are canceled. We see other people as our brothers and sisters in Christ.

Many sentimental ideas have been written and spoken about how men and women should get along with each other, despite differences in race, language, economic class, social background, education, sex, and the like. These are the distinctions, however, that are usually the raw material for individual and group defensiveness and aggressiveness. Triumphant faith means not simply that these differences are annulled historically, but rather that they are transcended through commitment to Jesus Christ.

When the crucifixion of Jesus has become the inward cross of our own experience, the words of Paul do not sound extravagant, but instead they seem like a plain statement of the truth: "I am crucified with Christ: nevertheless I live; yet not I, but Christ Jesus liveth in me: and the life I now live in the flesh I live by the faith of the Son of God, who loved me, and gave himself for me."

The death of Jesus on the cross did not cut him off from effective contact with men. Rather, it became the means through which his power to transform life was released into the world, so that men and women of the twentieth century can use Paul's words with the same reality to describe their own experience — not just in traditionally pious terms but as really illuminating their practical relationship to daily problems.

More significant than the growing influence of Jesus the teacher, transmitted through the wider circulation of his insights, and more important than the courageous example of Jesus the religious martyr, giving other people inspiration to stand for their convictions, is the effect of the living Christ today. The key to his transforming power is the inward cross.

The very act of killing Jesus, by which the world sought to dispose of him, became the means by which he was able to give men a new and more profound and more relentlessly realistic interpretation of what life is all about. All men everywhere ever since who have shared his personal approach to death in the midst of life have been made invulnerable to the assaults of fortune.

The cross was meant to end in death. It was meant to place an " iron curtain " between the condemned men and those who had rejected their influence and actions as evil. From the world's point of view, the affair on Calvary ended with the death of Jesus. No one in the crowd — not even the few who were personally loyal, and certainly not those who had arranged the trial and execution — would have dreamed that two thousand years later in every country under the sun millions of people would observe the anniversary of his death as the great dramatic occasion for refocusing the meaning of their own lives.

The way Jesus met his own death, in the last analysis, gave his impact upon men its final transforming and revolutionary power. His encounter with the eternal question mark before which all of us feel anxious and uncertain changed its meaning from defeat to victory. Paul caught the note accurately when he wrote to the Romans, "For I am persuaded, that neither death, nor life, nor angels, nor principalities, nor powers, nor things present, nor things to come, nor height, nor depth, nor any other creature, shall be able to separate us from the love of God, which is in Christ Jesus our Lord."

When we today, across the valley of centuries, watch the event on Calvary reach its conclusion, and hear Jesus say, " Father, into thy hands I commend my spirit," we hear words that not only show the attitude with which he accepted the end but also describe the spiritual basis for our dealing with the uncertain future. These final words from the cross are spoken to us with the intent that we should echo them in every decision that we are called upon to make, and in every relationship where we are seriously concerned.

The final words from the cross are from Psalm 31, and every first century Jew who heard them spoken would have known the frame of reference. Psalm 31 was used in Jesus' day as a hymn for the Feast of the Dedication in the Jerusalem Temple. It recalled to those who heard it the pollution of the sanctuary by order of Antiochus Epiphanes but a few generations earlier and the martyrdom of the faithful sons of Israel who had chosen to die rather than forswear their religious faith. The spirit of the feast is that God's righteous and eternal will shall prevail, regardless of what happens to us, and that in that knowledge we have confidence.

Someone has written that only a man and woman who are willing to die to themselves in order to be reborn in their children are able to qualify spiritually for parenthood. What more often happens, however, is that we tend to kill the personalities of our children, or at least distort them, in order to protect ourselves from the threats they give to our egos, and to save ourselves from inconveniences. Likewise, a successful marriage requires the willing death of the two young people concerned to the self-completeness of the single young adult in order to be reborn in partnership in a family. On no other terms is the conflict of wills transcended by a truly higher purpose. Or, once more, one cannot be creatively related to one's married children except by being willing to die to the pattern of being needed and deriving satisfaction thereby, in order to be reborn on a mature and adult level of mutuality. From the standpoint of mature living, every major crisis and decision of life involves using death as the measuring rod.

Physical death is actually a psychological symbol with wide application. The one thing we are sure about in regard to our own eventual decease is that nothing can be proved in advance, and this is why the symbol of death is so appropriate as the measure of any major adjustment or decision that we have to face. The happiness of one's marriage cannot be guaranteed in advance; neither can one's adequacy as a parent be simply taken for granted. There is no possible way of determining this year the outcome next year of American foreign policy.

We live in a world where circumstances force us to act before all the evidence is in. If we wait for complete assurance, we shall wait forever, and be merely ineffective human parasites carried along by affairs. On the other hand, creative living means accepting the symbol of death as the description of acting by faith, and then doing the best one can under the circumstances, trusting God even though one does not know all the answers.

Jesus on the cross used death as the measure of life — the acceptance of reality, first of all, not in blind resignation, but in creative trust; and then acting by a realistic evaluation of human nature. It is not within our power — since we are humans — to have complete understanding, complete command, complete virtue. We can only do the best we can with what we have, where we are. The fullness and completeness of life is not given into our management. Yet, in that portion which is ours to use, we are indeed partners of the Most High, if we make that partnership a living reality by admitting the facts and then going ahead to do what we can here, trusting God for the rest — provided only that we are honest with ourselves and sincere in our efforts.

Many of us were thrilled by the wartime message of King George VI of England at Christmas after Dunkirk. Quoting from M. Louise Haskins, the king read over the radio to the beleaguered British people: " 'I said to the man who stood at the gate of the year, " Give me a light that I may tread safely into the unknown," and he replied, " Go out into the darkness and put your hand into the hand of God. That shall be to you better than light and safer than a known way." ' "

It was in this spirit that the three-hour drama of Calvary reached its conclusion. Quoting from The Psalms, that treasury of Hebrew devotion and religious insight, Jesus ended his struggle on the cross with the words of the ancient hymn: " Into thine hand I commit my spirit: thou hast redeemed me, O Lord God of truth." As far as that one episode within history was concerned, it was over with his death; but as far as the judgment and redemption of history were concerned a new power was unleashed in the world.

With the death of Jesus, the drama of the cross did not end, but its stage was changed. It was moved from the geographical site of Calvary, a small hill outside Jerusalem, to the heart of every man, woman, or child who seeks to understand the meaning of his own life and to clarify his relationships with other people on the most realistic level.

The cross was outward on the original Good Friday. It stood over against the men who saw it, outside their lives, something to which they were related only as spectators. With the death of Jesus in the spirit of confident victory, the cross was made inward for every man, woman, and child who is discontent with being a spectator in the game of life, and would participate in honesty and truth.

When you and I, as the drama of Calvary is played to the conclusion, contemplate the cross, we see either the stark evidence of a tragedy that is over or we see the creative symbol of a new power and vision in which we can share. If we see only an outward cross, we see only the former; but if the cross has become an inward reality in our own hearts, then we see the latter, not just in theory but in fact.

The inward cross means that I am a new man, living in a new world, because Jesus Christ died for me that I might live today by his spirit, related to my brethren by a common faith built upon his foundation. It means that I am ready to accept death as the measure of life, going ahead with confidence in the purpose of God, provided I share the humility of the cross. It means that this tortured world in which I live has a hope that cannot be betrayed, if once it is understood for what it is meant to be. It means that you and I may live now by triumphant faith.